For our grandchildren

Best wishes
Margaret Moore

This book belongs to

....

....

The Big Book
of Poems
for Little People

Written by Margaret Moore
Illustrated by Chris French

skycat
publications
www.skycatpublications.com

ISBN 978 0 9927451 6 5

British Library Cataloguing-in-Publication Data
A catalogue record for this book is available from the British Library.

1st edition published in 2010 by Book Guild Publishing

This 2nd edition published in the UK by Skycat Publications
Vaiseys Farm, Cock Lane, Brent Eleigh, Sudbury, Suffolk CO10 9PA
Tel 01787 248476
info@skycatpublications.com

Printed in England by Lavenham Press Ltd
47 Water Street, Lavenham, Suffolk CO10 9RN
Tel 01787 249215

Typeset in OpenDyslexic 16pt

To children everywhere.
Imagined moments. Forever memories.

Contents

Books by the same Author

Short Poems for Little People   Book Guild Publishing (1st ed.)
Almost Full Circle 2014   Skycat Publications

FOR OTHER BOOKS BY SKYCAT PUBLICATIONS VISIT
www.skycatpublications.com

TWO FEET TALL

I see the World from two feet tall
Which isn't very tall at all.
I met a dog the other day
Who sees the World in the same way.

My granddad likes to sleep a lot
When he sits in his chair.
I wondered why that happened
Every time that he sat there.

I looked around the back of it
And looked under the seat
But there was nothing to be seen
To make him go to sleep.

Perhaps when I am very old
When I'm at least fifteen.
I'll find out how the snooze
                chair works
And what makes
granddad dream.

GRANDDAD

SHARING

I'm always told that I must share,
It's what you have to do.
I'm not quite sure how sharing works,
I need some sort of clue.
My teacher said you let your friends
Take turns when you play games.
So that's what sharing means to us,
I don't know why they made a fuss.

WHISTLING

I thought I'd learn to whistle,
It seemed a lot of fun.
My uncle said he'd show me how it could be done.
I pushed my lips quite forward
        and tried to twist my tongue.
But when I did a great big blow,
A whistle didn't come.

THE BIRTHDAY CAKE

The birthday cake sat on the plate.
It looked all nice and scrummy.
I thought I'd try a little bit to make sure it was yummy.
I only took a little bit to see if I was right.
And yes, it was, it tasted good.
I took another bite.
My sister came into the room and said
'You've had your share'
I stamped my foot and got quite cross and shouted
'That's not fair'.

WOBBLY TEETH

I've had a wobbly tooth all week,
It is a bother when I eat.
My friend came round to play with me.
Mum said that he could stay for tea.
He's lost a lot of teeth you know,
And so he has to eat quite slow.
When our big teeth decide to come,
Our teatime treats will be more fun.

GRANDMA

Why do grandmas always do
Things like hugging and kissing you?
Why can't they be more like us
And say 'Hello' without a fuss?

5

WHERE ARE BABY'S TEETH?

I think our baby's lost her teeth
I can't see where they are.
Perhaps she does what granddad does
and keeps them in a jar.

QUESTIONS

I ask a lot of questions,
I always want to know,
I can be quite a nuisance,
Because they told me so.

If I don't ask these questions
I will never know.
I'll have to be a nuisance
But that's already so.

WHAT IS A BRIDESMAID?

I'm going to be a bridesmaid,
My aunty told me so.
I don't know what a bridesmaid is
but said I'd have a go.
I get to wear a nice pink frock
and carry lots of flowers.
To me it's just like dressing up.
I play that game for hours.

THE HOLIDAY

My bucket and spade are important to me.
I am going away today you see.
My bag is packed.
My swimsuit is ready.
I've got some sweets and I'm taking teddy.
I jump up and down and shout "Hooray"
I like to go on holiday.

FOOTPRINTS IN THE SAND

Where have my footprints gone in the sand?
Has the tide taken them to another land?
They were there on the beach when I left yesterday.
But now they are somewhere far away.

GROWN-UPS

Why do grown-ups always shout
The minute that you run about?
'Don't do that or you'll fall over'
Is what they shout, because they're older.
I shout back 'Just you wait and see'
then fall down and cut my knee.

THE WINDY DAY

I wanted to go out today
but was afraid I'd blow away.
They said the wind was very strong,
I couldn't see it they must be wrong.

I stood outside the door to see.
The wind blew hard and frightened me.
I ran back in and shut the door.
I will stay in and play some more.

GRANDMA'S HOUSE

I bounce upon the bed a lot
and run around the house.
And Grandma doesn't say
'Be quiet as a mouse'.
She laughs at me and then joins in.
We have a lot of fun.
I'm glad I came to Grandma's house.
She likes it when I come.

MY SHADOW

I've got a shadow, my dad told me so.
It's always around wherever I go.
It's there in the sunshine but not in the rain.
I'll have to watch carefully when it comes out again.

THE FIRST BIG SANDCASTLE

The castle that I made today
is very big and grand.
I made it on the beach with dad
and lots and lots of sand.

I put some shells and stones on it
and made a flag as well.
I sat and looked at my hard work
but then I had to yell.
The sea was rushing over it
and spoiling all my fun.
I had worked hard to make
it stay.
But it was washed away
today.

I thought I'd call our baby Zacharia Small,
Mum seemed to choose a lot of names
I didn't like at all.
She came home with our baby
All new and pink and small.
But when I took a closer look
She's not a Zak at all!

OUR
BABY'S
NAME

IS IT A LONG WAY?

How far is far away?
They never seem to say.
Is it passed the corner shop?
Is that the place where I should stop?
I went right passed the shop today.
It didn't seem too far away.

THE STAIRS

My sister climbed up on the stairs
and had a nasty tumble.
As she's so small and she can't speak
she couldn't even grumble.

MY BEDROOM BUS

My bunk bed is a bus today.
My passengers are on top.
My steering wheel is a saucepan lid.
I've got a bell to ring when I stop.
My teddies like to ride with me.
As we drive along there's lots to see.
My bedroom bus drives far away.
Perhaps I'll ride out another day.

WRITING

I wrote my name at school today.
It was the very first time.
My teacher said I'd done quite well.
The writing was just fine.
I showed my mum and grandma too.
They said it was quite neat.
As I had been a clever boy,
For tea I'd have a treat.
I hope my writing stays the same,
So I can have more treats again.

THE LONDON TRIP

I went up to London but didn't see the Queen.
I thought she would come out and ask me where I'd been.
I went up in the London Eye and nearly touched the sky.
I stood upon a great big ship and watched the World go by.
I was puffed out with things to see,
And was quite pleased we stopped for tea.

PINK SPIDERS

I am afraid of spiders.
They are so fast and black.
Perhaps, if they were pink instead.
I'd like them better like that.

THE JOURNEY

When we go out in the car
I always hope we don't go far.
I get fed up just sitting there
They point things out, I stare and stare.
But all I ask is 'Are we there?'

I sit, I fidget, I moan and groan.
I do this until we get home.
They let me out, I run and shout.
I don't know why they take me out.

RAINING

Do you know where the rain comes from?
It comes out of the sky.
My dad says it's a nuisance,
And so I asked him why.

He said it always makes a mess
And he prefers it dry.
I don't think I have ever seen
Dry rain come from the sky.

WHAT DO BABIES DO?

Our baby doesn't seem quite right,
He sleeps all day and cries all night.
He doesn't use a knife and fork
He never plays and he can't walk.
I thought when I was told he'd come
He would be a lot more fun.

FLOWERS

Where are all the flowers from
that were in the shops today.
They are usually in a garden
and always seem to stay.
Is there someone naughty
who takes them all away?
I don't know if she'll get told off
but mum bought some today.

GRANDDAD'S BIRTHDAY

My Granddad has a birthday soon.
He's very, very old.
I bought him a red scarf to wear
because he's always cold.
He's going to have a great big cake
with candles on the top.
I think that as he's very old,
there will be quite a lot.

WHAT IS A DREAM?

A dream is something like a light.
They come in the night when my eyes are shut tight.
The light is switched off so that I can find dreams.
I keep thinking about the places I've been.
My dreams are just mine and secret to me.
And that is exactly how dreams should be.

We've got a baby in the house,
I am as quiet as a mouse.
They hide him under lots of clothes,
All I can see is his small nose.

THE NEW ARRIVAL

They say that he is going to be
Another handful, just like me.
I don't know what they mean at all.
My hands, I think, are still quite small.

AN AUNTY

If you have an aunty, I don't know what you get.
I'm told I've got an aunty
But I haven't seen it yet.
Is it something in a glass or is it in a box?
Whatever it turns out to be, they tell me I've got lots.

NEW SHOES

My little sister wears no shoes,
She doesn't even talk.
She cries a bit and crawls around,
She doesn't even walk.
I brought my new shoes home with me
And showed my little sister.
I can't tell if she likes my shoes, but even so I told her
If she grows big and starts to walk,
she can have some when she's older.

LEARNING
TO SKIP

I tried to learn to skip today.
My feet kept getting in the way.
I tried a jump and then a hop.
I did some more and didn't stop.
I am so pleased my feet found out
how to hop and skip about.

THE HOSPITAL VISIT

I had to visit the hospital.
My friend is very sick.
He told me that he can't go home
and must stay for a bit.
I asked him what the problem was.
He said he needs some time
to get the medicine from the nurse.
And then he'll be just fine.
I hope my friend will be home soon.
I've already bought him a big balloon.
I said a prayer to make him well.
But mum said only time will tell.

MY LITTLE SISTER

I look after my sister as she is only three.
Because I am four,
I know a lot more,
so she looks up to me.

When I look after my sister,
I have to open the door.
Because she can't reach the handle,
until she's at least four.

LEARNING

When I was a baby, I had to learn to talk.
When I was a toddler, I had to learn to walk.
Now that I am three years old
I chat and run about,
But find that I am being told
'Sit still and do not shout'.

MY LITTLE BROTHER

With one foot going one way
And one foot going the other.
I laughed and watched the antics
Of my little brother.
He tried to do a cartwheel
and then he tried another.
I do enjoy the antics of my little brother.

CHOICES

Why can't I find just what I want
It shouldn't be too hard?
I only came into the shop to pick a birthday card.

My friend is five years old you know
And he likes great big cards.
I can't find one I think he'll like, it really is quite hard.

Perhaps I'll buy him sweets instead
They've got some that I like.
I'm sure he'll like some sweets instead.
Yes, that sounds quite all right.

I went to bed the other night
and it was still quite light.
I shut my eyes and snuggled down
and all seemed quite all right.
I had a dream that woke me up.
It was about the night.
I wish the dark would go away.
It gave me quite a fright.

NIGHT TIME

THE HAIRCUT

I have to have my hair cut now that I
    am three.
I don't want my hair cut.
It seems all right to me.
Mum said I'm going to nursery
and it will make me smart.
If that's what going to nursery means.
I don't think I will start.

Our baby she does dreadful things,
She doesn't use her pot.
She doesn't tell us when she's been,
She does this quite a lot.
I don't think it is very nice.
The other day she did this twice!

DID I DO THAT?

THE TELEPHONE

The telephone rang, I thought I'd see
who was trying to speak to me.
I picked it up and said 'Hello'
There was a voice I did not know.
The voice said 'Just who can that be?'
I said 'Oh! silly, it is me.'

THE WORM

I went into the garden and found a worm today.
I put him with the flowers to keep the birds away.
My Dad said birds eat worms and things.
I hope they don't find mine.
I'll visit him another day to see if he is fine.

THE NAUGHTY STEP

We have a naughty step at home.
I'm sure we didn't buy it.
It was here when we moved in.
I don't think I will try it.
My friend said he has one as well.
But his one is worn out.
As he's my friend I said "that's fine".
On naughty days he can use mine.

WHERE'S THAT CAT?

My cat got lost the other day.
I hoped he wasn't far away.
We searched and looked inside and out.
While in the garden I gave a shout.
"Where are you Dylan?" because that's his name.
And suddenly he came home again.

IN A MUDDLE

Hats and coats are all right,
Gloves and shoes are fine,
But when I change at school sometimes,
I wonder where are mine.

I nearly always get it wrong
and come home in a muddle.
I can't help it if I find
The whole thing too much trouble.

THE MOUSE

I lost my mouse the other day
I thought he had got clean away.
My sister went into her room,
There was a scream heard on the Moon.
I rushed into her room at speed
And told her there just was no need
To shout and scream and rant and rave
And popped him back into his cage.

POCKET MONEY

Pocket money sounds like fun.
I hope my Dad will give me some.
I'll help to put my toys away.
I'll tidy my room at the end of the day.
Maybe I'll eat some peas today.
Maybe I'll even do as they say.
Yes, pocket money sounds like fun.
I'm looking forward to getting some.

The sky is very dark at night.
There's only stars to make it bright.
They seem to be just everywhere.
I wonder if there's hundreds there.
I hope they'll twinkle all night long.
The day will come and they'll be gone.

STARS AT NIGHT

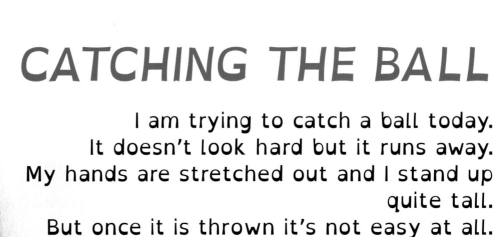

CATCHING THE BALL

I am trying to catch a ball today.
It doesn't look hard but it runs away.
My hands are stretched out and I stand up
quite tall.
But once it is thrown it's not easy at all.
No, I don't like this game.
I will just play football.

RED SLIPPERS

I've got some new red slippers,
I keep them in their box,
I think they're rather special,
I like them lots and lots.

I haven't put them on yet,
I keep them on my bed,
I just like seeing my slippers,
All fluffy, new and red.

SHOPPING

We walk down to the bus stop,
We get up on the bus.
We do all of our shopping without a lot of fuss.

But then I think that I am bored
And start to moan and groan,
Which means I get some sweeties which last until I get home.

I know I shouldn't do it, I know it is not right,
But that's what makes the shopping trip
More than just all right.

I know I saw it on the chair,
I've looked and looked just everywhere.
I'm trying to think where I have been,
It's been some time since we came in.
I don't think I can search some more,
I can't think what I'm looking for.

WHERE IS IT?

TIME

I'm learning to tell the time with Mum.
She shows me how it can be done.
The sticks that move she said are hands.
I don't think Mum quite understands.
What is time?
I cannot see it.
I've lots to do, can't spare a minute.
Perhaps I'll learn another day.
Time seems to have raced away.

THE SECRET

I don't know what a secret is,
but my friend says she's got one.
Perhaps if I am good today,
my Mum will let me buy some.
My Mum said secrets can't be bought.
They're things that only I know
And no one else can have them
unless you tell them so.

HELPING DAD

I sometimes wash the car with Dad.
I help him lots and he's quite glad.
I splash the water all about.
I get quite wet and laugh and shout.
The car gets clean and so do I.
Then Mum calls out
"It's time to get dry".

WHILE MUM'S AWAY

While mum was in hospital
dad took great care of me.
We had all sorts of strange things for
our dinner and our tea.
We had some chips and beans and
things
And then we had some more.
I'm glad mum's back home again
with dinners as before.

TOO
HIGH

Why is everything so big?
it really isn't fair,
To reach the cakes and buns and things
I have to use a chair.

LOST AND FOUND

My Granddad made a funny face and tried to make me smile.
I told him I was sad today and would be for a while.
He asked me what the trouble was and what could be
so bad.
I said I'd lost my pencil case and
hadn't told Mum or Dad.
He said it wasn't lost at all and
knew where we could find it.
He moved the cushion on the
chair and said it had been hiding
there.
I am so glad my Granddad came.
Because he made me smile again.

TWINS

I've got two friends who look the same.
My Mum said they are twins.
The trouble is when we play games
I can't tell which one wins.
I said I didn't understand
how can they be the same?
Two babies grow instead of one
and are together when they come.
My Mum said a twin is much more fun.
You get two friends instead of one.

THE MYSTERY

It's round and sort of fluffy.
It's big and sort of soft.
It's got three legs and rocks a bit.
I found it in our loft.
No one knows about it.
Goodness knows where it is from.
I don't know what it's supposed to be.
But I think it's rather fun.

THE GRUMBLY MIDGE

I saw a Grumbly Midge.
He likes to raid our fridge.
Some days he eats and never stops.
I found him eating my ice pops.
I told him my dad says it's me.
He really must now let him see.
I'm not the one who's telling fibs.
There really is a Grumbly Midge.

I THOUGHT
I LOST
IT

When I was two, I lost a shoe.
When I was three, I found it.
Now I am four, it fits no more.
So who cares now about it?

PRINCESS

I ought to be a princess.
My Daddy told me so.
I'd like a crown that sparkles
and a dress with a big pink bow.
My slippers could be silver.
My necklace could be gold.
Sometimes I could be naughty
And not do as I'm told.
My Daddy says a princess is always very good.
If a princess has to be like that
I don't think that I could.
A princess doesn't sound much fun.
So now I don't want to be one.

FEELING UNWELL

I went to visit my Grandma
because she said she's not well.
I asked her what the trouble was
but she said she could not tell.
She said she felt a bit wobbly.
She said she felt a bit hot.
I said I felt like that as well
if I run and do not stop.
I think I know what her problem is
it's when she goes down to the shops.
She rushes around with her trolley
and doesn't take time to stop.

GRANDDAD'S HAIR

'Where has granddad's hair gone?'
I asked my mum today.
She said he used to have a lot
But it has worn away.
I wonder if it is because
He wears a cap all day.
My friend he wears a cap at
school but his hair
seems to stay.

TEN

Why do we have ten fingers?
Why do we have ten toes?
Why do we need so many?
I don't think anyone knows.

I try to use mine all at once
And always get in a muddle.
I think whoever invented me
Has caused me a lot of trouble.

MY TUMMY

I've got a big fat tummy,
They say it's too much food.
As that is what a tummy's for,
I think they're rather rude.

BUTTONS

I'm trying to do my buttons up,
my shirt has got so many.
I told my Mum I need a shirt
that simply doesn't have any.
She said I've nearly managed it
and soon I'll get it right.
I don't think my Mum understands
I'll be trying to do them all night.

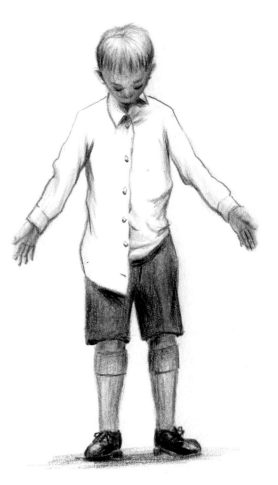

IT'S DARK
AT NIGHT

I'm trying to stop the dark at night
when I go up to bed.
Mum says it's when the day is done
and the moon comes out instead.
I said if I keep looking up
will the day stay there a bit longer?
She said it can't, it has to go.
so that the moon can start to glow.

THE SURPRISE

I went to bed the other night
And all seemed quite OK
But when I woke my daddy said
'Just come and see what's in this bed.'
I peered and peered and I did see
A little sister, just like me.

My mummy said she came to us
Because she was just ready.
I went and got a gift for her,
I gave her my old teddy.

FEELING BETTER NOW

They said I was going to see grandma,
So I got dressed and in the car.
I hoped the journey would be quick,
But soon I started feeling sick.
I said I couldn't wait some more
And was quite sick upon the floor.

THE DAY HAS A FRIEND

Where does the day go when it ends?
I'm sure it must have lots of friends.
I like it when it's bright and warm.
I run and hide if there's a storm.

If rain comes down I sit and frown
Because my friends don't come around.
I think it has a friend called Moon
'Cos when it's gone, I find my room
Is bright and silver with its glow.
Oh! That's the place where day must go.

54

THE BEARD

My friend's Dad has got a beard.
I don't know how he got it.
Did it grow as he got old?
Perhaps he couldn't stop it.
If he does what Daddy does
and shaves his face each day.
He'll find that very, very soon
his beard has gone away.

THE DENTIST

I'm going to see the Dentist
now that I'm five years old.
He said it is very important
I brush my teeth when I'm told.
I gave him a smile and told him
I would like my teeth to stay.
The only thing wrong with that is
The tooth fairy stays away.

MY LITTLE SISTER'S PARTY

My sister wants a party.
She's two years old today.
Because she's only little
she doesn't know what to say.
I'll tell my Mum what she would like.
I'm sure it's loads of toys.
Her party can have all my friends.
She wouldn't want any boys.
There's lots of things that she could choose.
She'd like a doll and shiny shoes.
Good job I'm here to help her out.
It's what a big sister is all about.

FEELING POORLY

What is a cough?
It is not nice.
What is a cold?
It's sniffy.
What is the point of both of these?
You just feel tired and squiffy.

NOT MUCH FUN

Learning to do things at school
Isn't very much fun at all.
They want me to learn how to write,
I said I wouldn't, but then I might.
To learn to read seems hard to do,
The words all seem a jumble too.
I'm four years old and I don't need
To learn to write or learn to read!

MY PET

I had a fish called Fred
But now that he is dead.
I have a cat called Ben,
So now I'm happy again.

My uncle came to visit
and brought a kite for me.
I don't know how you make it work.
I'll have to wait and see.
He said we need a windy day
because that makes it fly.

THE
KITE

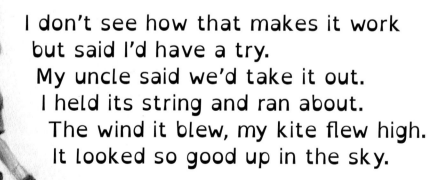

I don't see how that makes it work
but said I'd have a try.
My uncle said we'd take it out.
I held its string and ran about.
The wind it blew, my kite flew high.
It looked so good up in the sky.

CHANGE OF NAME

My friend he changed his name today.
I thought his name was here to stay.
When he was born he was called Tom.
But now he wants me to call him Ron.
I think I might change my name too.
I'd like to be known as Scooby Doo.

THE ALPHABET

I'm learning to say the alphabet.
ABC and lots more.
They are the letters that make the words.
I'm told that's what they are for.
My teacher will help me get them right.
She says I am getting quite good.
I can't be sure I will learn them all.
But if I can, I said I would.

WHO IS THAT?

I look into the mirror and what do I see?
A person who is dressed exactly like me.
I don't know how a mirror works,
I know it isn't magic.
I only know it works each time.
I think my mirror is rather fine.

MY FIRST DAY

I'm off to school, it's my first day.
If I don't like it, I won't stay.
My bag is packed, my coat is on.
I hope I won't be gone for long.

My mum says I must be quite brave.
I blow a kiss and give a wave.
I got as far as the front door
And found I worried more and more.
I cried a bit and, on the way,
Thought I'd stay at home today.

WAITING

To ride a bike you need to be
a bit older than just three,
So when I'm four I hope to say,
"Watch me while I race away".

GRANDMA'S SPECIAL CAT

My Grandma has a special cat
he follows her around the flat.
When she is out he likes to sleep
and then he has something to eat.
He jumps up on the window sill
and looks outside while sitting still.
When she comes home he wants to play.
My Grandma's cat is fun each day.

TONSILS

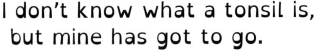

I don't know what a tonsil is,
but mine has got to go.
Dad said it makes my throat quite
  sore.
  I told him, "Yes, I know".
  I have to go to hospital and stay
  there overnight.
  I'll have a sleep and when I wake
  my throat will be all right.
  The Doctor took my tonsil out
  while I was having a dream.
  To make my throat feel nice
again,
I'll have to eat lots of ice cream.

GREENS

I'm growing up fast they tell me,
I'm eating my meals each day.
But as fast as I eat my dinners,
The greens don't go away.

I'm doing my best to please them.
I even ate peas today.
My friend doesn't eat all his dinners,
And as far as I know he's OK.

SO CROSS

I was so cross I'd been told off
I thought I'd run away.
I packed my bag and strutted off
I thought I'd go that day.

I went straight down the
garden path
But heard along the way,
There's cake for tea with
buns and things.
I'll leave another day.

THE MAGICIAN

I don't know what a magician is,
but I'm going to see one today.
Daddy says they do magic,
and make things go away.
I wonder if I asked him
he could show me how it works.
I've got a sore knee that's a bother,
and it really, really hurts.

SPORTS DAY

We're having a sports day at school very soon.
I've been practising running all afternoon.
My teacher said we will have races to run.
There'll be hoops to run through.
It all sounds good fun.
At the end of the day we'll find out who won.

COOKING WITH MUM

I want to bake some cakes with mum.
She's going to show me how it's done.
There's eggs and flour and sugar and milk.
I whiz it all around and make sure none is spilt.
I pour it all into the tins which is fun.

They go into the oven until they
are done.
When mum took them out,
they looked good to me.
And so we both ate them for our
tea.

BATHTIME

I like to bath and splash about
The water makes me shout.
But just as I enjoy myself
It's time that I got out.

BUBBLES

There's nothing that can make
me laugh
Quite like having a bubble bath.
The water froths and bubbles up
I scoop and pour it from a cup.
My face is pink and it would seem
It is the best way to get clean.

THE SPIDER

A spider ran across the floor
And hid beneath the kitchen door.
My brother he came with a cup
And tried to scoop the spider up.
We looked and searched without a sound,
The spider just could not be found.
I think his legs raced him away,
We'll probably see him another day.

WHO HAS GOT IT?

My uncle lost his temper,
I don't know where it is.
I heard him tell my aunty
She'd got him in a tizz.

I looked under the cushions
But could not find it there.
I don't know where his temper is,
Can't find it anywhere.

THE PROMISE

I said I would be good today.
I would tidy my room and put things away.
I said I would promise, because that's what you do.
But what is a promise, I don't have a clue?
My sister she promises all sorts of things.
She tries to please mum.
Is that what it means?
I'm told if you promise, you do as you say.
Because a promise is special
and not just for that day.

GRANDMA'S JEWELLERY BOX

My grandma has got a jewellery box.
It's full of treasures, there's lots and lots.
The shiny brooches look nice on me.
There are rings that might fit.
I'll have to wait and see.
When I'm all dressed up, I look like a princess.
I think grandma's jewellery is really the best.

THE ANGRY BOFF

My teddy he needs mending,
His ear has been pulled off.
It wasn't me that did it,
It was an angry Boff.

An angry Boff is someone
Who breaks things when they're cross.
As I don't lose my temper,
It was the angry Boff.

FULL UP

We went to tea, my friend and me, it was a special treat.
We'd been good boys and made no noise,
Our good had lasted all week.
We ate and ate, our cheeks were full,
We felt all big and round.
We ate so much that we both thought
Our tummies would hit the ground.
When we stood up, we rocked a bit,
We thought we would fall over.
We liked our tea, my friend and me
But are glad that it's all over.

THE ODD DOG

I know a dog who is very odd
He doesn't bark at all.
He climbs up trees just like a cat
And goes to sleep upon the mat.
I wonder how he got like that.

THE GLOVES

My gloves have got some finger bits.
But I can't get it right.
My fingers always go in wrong.
I find that it just takes too long.
My fingers want to wriggle about.
They don't need gloves, I take them out.
If I find my hands get quite cold.
Mum said I'll wish I'd done as I'm told.

THE SPELLING
TEST

When I go to school today,
I'm going to do my best.
My teacher told me it was time to have a little test.
I had to write down lots of words
to see if I could spell.
I tried my best and got them right,
so mum said I'd have a treat tonight.
For tea I could have whatever I liked.

FLOATING

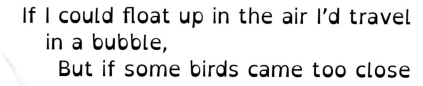

If I could float up in the air I'd travel
in a bubble,
But if some birds came too close
by I think I'd be in trouble.
They'd probably peck and
poke at it to see if it was
food,
And as I'm quite a big boy
now I'd tell them they were
rude.
A bubble doesn't last too long
and so it's best I stay,
Down on the ground for some time
yet and fly another day.

CATCHING

My friend he sneezed and coughed a bit,
I thought it rather funny,
until I found the next day that my nose was rather runny.
I told my friend and he said that if I had asked for more.
He would have passed his cold to me,
cos that's what friends are for.

I DON'T THINK SO

It was time to go but I said 'No'
I really didn't want to.
Why do I have to stop my fun
Just as it has begun?

WORDS

I've got a book with pictures in
And lots and lots of words.
As I can't read I think it is
wonderfully absurd.

THE LOST SHOE

I wonder what you have to do
If you're two and lost a shoe.
I had it on when we came out.
We've done some shopping and been about.

I don't know where my shoe has gone.
My mum asked 'Has it been gone long?'
I don't know what they're worried about.
I never walk when we are out!

FIGHTING

I got a smack, it wasn't right,
All I did was start the fight.
I didn't punch or kick at all,
I only pushed him so he'd fall.

His mother came and so did mine,
they asked a lot and then said,
'Fine, if you can't play without a row,
you'll both go home with us right now.'

WHAT IS A NEIGHBOUR?

Dad said we've got new neighbours.
He said he was very pleased.
I wonder what a neighbour is.
Is it something that we need?
I looked inside the cupboard
and looked inside the fridge.
I just can't find them anywhere.
They must be very big.
Dad said I would be seeing them
when they come in to tea.
I found out they are people.
Just like me!

KNITTING

I saw a lot of balls of wool
and what looked like some sticks.
I asked my gran what they were for
and were they to do tricks?

She laughed and said they are to knit
and make things you can wear.
I had a go and dropped a stitch,
can't find it anywhere.
I think it must have
disappeared into the air.

HANDS AND FEET

I have two hands, one left, one right,
I have two feet the same.
I don't know where they all came from,
They were with me when I came.

THE SHOE SHOP

I saw a shop full up with shoes.
I thought a shoe was hard to lose.
If all the shoes I saw were lost.
There are a lot of grown-ups, cross.

When I have a cold, they say I have a chill.
When I say I've had enough, they say 'Well are
you ill?'
If I have a little cough, they ask me why I did it.
I tell them I don't have a clue, so off to bed I
go, with flu!

WHAT HAVE YOU GOT?

MEASLES

Do you want my measles?
Do you want my spots?
You will have to bring a bag,
Because there are lots and lots.

When I look down, I see my feet,
They stop me falling over.
Why is it then that when I'm out
They can be such a bother?

TRIPPING UP

THINKING

What is a pet?
It can be anything you like.
A pet for me would have to be
quite tough and quick and bright.
I think a dog, quite big and strong
might be just right for me.
I'll have to think about it though
because it's time for tea.

NOT A GOOD DAY

When I woke up I thought I'd be
very good this morning.
But things went wrong and so I found
by noon I'd had a warning.
By teatime I had had a smack
so that was quite the end of that.

BILLY

I have a friend no one can see,
He's always there and talks to me.
Some people say that I am silly
When I have chats with my friend Billy.

My mum says they don't really know
That my friend Billy will one day go
And when I'm older I will find
That my friend Billy was in my mind.

NO 'ONCE UPON A TIME.'

Why do all my stories start
'Once upon a time'?
I want to write a story and say that it is mine.
My story will begin at home,
I'll talk about my toys.
I'll tell you that my friends come around.
But I don't want any boys.
When my story is finished,
I'll make a little book.
There is no 'Once upon a time',
I like to think my book is fine.

THE X-RAY

Have you had an X-Ray?
I had one today.
I had it at the hospital,
but didn't have to stay.
An X-Ray is a picture
of bones and your insides.
The Doctor showed me my one.
It helps him to decide.
I hurt my arm at school today.
He had to make quite sure
my arm bone was not broken.
It was just very, very sore.

SINK OR SWIM

My dad said I should learn to swim
So off we went and I plunged in.
I thought that I would, like a boat
have no trouble in staying afloat.

I found that I was sinking fast
I knew that this just couldn't last.
My dad he grabbed me by the shoulder,
Perhaps I'll swim when I am older.

TRYING
AND
TYING

I'm trying to tie a bow today,
I've tried to tie it in every way.
I twist it, I tie it, I pull it, I turn.
I simply can't do it.
I will never learn.

THE WELLIES

I have a pair of wellies,
They're big and new and green.
I put them on the other day
To walk in by the stream.
I thought I ought to try them out
And went to find a puddle.
I walked into a muddy mess
And now I am in trouble.

SOCKS AND SHOES

I know my shoes are dirty,
I know my socks look grey,
But when I take them off at night
They seem to fly away.
I stayed awake the other night
To see if I was right and,
Yes, I was, in came my mum
With fresh ones, nice and bright.

HIDING

I know that I am shy, but I don't know why.
I always want to hide away
when anybody comes to stay.
I find the best place here to hide
is by dad's chair, so big and wide.
I might come out when they have gone.
I just hope they don't stay too long.

MY READING GLASSES

I need to wear some glasses
to help me read my books.
Mum said I could choose some
to see how I would look.
I didn't like to wear them,
they seemed a nuisance to me.
But when I found some shiny ones
I looked in the mirror to see.
I think I look so pretty.
I'm glad that they are mine.
I don't know why I was worried.
My glasses look just fine.

BUBBLES

Where do all the bubbles go when they float
  down to the ground?
    One minute they are there
      and then they can't be found.
     I've got some bubble mixture
    which makes them fly up high.
     But when I try to catch them, they burst,
  I don't know why.
Perhaps if I am gentle
I'll catch them as they go by.

OOZLE

The Oozle Doozle bird flies very high,
He often has chats with the pilots who fly.
He is always careful to keep well away,
When an aircraft is cruising to your holiday.
But should you look out and see Oozle go by,
Please give him a wave as he cruises on high.

THE BIRTHDAY PARTY

My birthday party was alright,
I even managed to have a fight.
One of the boys who came to it
Thought he'd be tough and barge a bit.
I told him he could not do that
And when he did, I struck him back.
We pulled and tugged upon the ground,
until finally my mum came round.
She stood us up and made us say
'Let's be friends and find a way
To play some games without a fight'
Then friends can visit another night.

WISHING

Do you know how to make a wish?
I can't seem to get it right.
I close my eyes and frown a bit
I keep them shut really tight.
I've seen a doll that I'd very much like
But my wishing is not going well.
If you make a wish it can sometimes come true
But remember you must not tell.

BOSSY BOOTS

My friend calls me bossy boots
I don't know why that is.
I try to sort the games all out.
But he says some are his.
I like to tell him what to do.
Then he says that's not right.
We then get cross and shout a lot.
Which ends up with a fight.

THE BABY

My friends mum is having a baby.
She looks very strange and quite fat.
My friend said the baby will be here next week.
I am wondering just how he knows that.
He said his mum told him the baby is ready to
come out to see who I am.
So I'll visit next week with a present
And tell it that my name is Sam.

THE UMBLY BUMBLY

The Umbly Bumbly is stupid and big.
He lives in a kennel but eats like a pig.
He doesn't wear shoes and he doesn't use money.
He just loves to play and roll on his tummy.

WHO CAN FLY?

I saw a bee go buzzing by.
I thought it must be fun to fly.
I stood upon the bathroom stool
And jumped and flapped until I did fall.
No, flying is no fun at all.

THE HOOVER

My mum has got a big machine
that makes a lot of noise.
She keeps it in the cupboard
away from little boys.
It has a lot of pipes and things
and also has a door.
A light comes on when she plugs in,
I asked her what it's for.
She told me it is to clear up
the mess that people make,
Especially when little boys
eat lots and lots of cake.

THE WALKING STICK

My granddad's got a walking stick.
It takes him for a walk.
When he goes out he meets his friends.
He sometimes stops to talk.
Before he had his walking stick he
stayed around the house.
But now his stick takes him for walks
he's always out and about.

THE BEST SANDCASTLE

We built a great big castle
We made it out of sand.
We're on the beach on holiday
Our castle is quite grand.
We put some shells upon it
that made it look so good.
But the waves will soon wash it away.
from where it proudly stood.

FRIENDSHIP

Yesterday I had a friend.
Today he doesn't like me.
Tomorrow who knows how he'll be.
I'll just have to wait and see.

WAITING TO GROW

What can be the matter with me
I'd really like to know.
I eat my meals and stretch a lot
But simply do not grow.
My dad told me it is because
I'm in a great big hurry.
I'll grow a little bit each day
And so I shouldn't worry.

THE SEASIDE SHOP

We're in a seaside shop today.
My granddad says we're far away.
I've seen a shop that is so small.
It sells some shells and that's not all.
It has some buckets and some spades.
There are sunhats and also shades.
This seaside shop sells balls and kites.
They've got rubber crabs that give me a fright.
I'll have to think what I should get.
I might just buy a fishing net.
I am so very glad we came.
We'll have to visit here again.

MOVING HOUSE

When you move house, I'm not sure what you do.
Is there some place that you take everything to?
Mum says my toys will all be packed up.
I've got so many things, we will need a big truck.
My bike is quite big and my scooter needs room.
My new house is ready, we'll be going there soon.
I hope I will like it.
It might take some time.
But I'll make some new friends.
And that will be fine.

LETTERS

Where does the postman find all his letters?
He always has lots in his bag.
I never get letters when he comes around,
They are always for my dad.
He said perhaps grandma could write
to me
she could tell me about all her news.
I could find out what she's been doing
because she could give me some clues.

THE TRAIN JOURNEY

I'm going on a train today.
The train can take you far away.
There's lots to see as we go by.
I can't see the road and wondered why.
My daddy said the train needs a track.
They are like big lines that sound
clickerty clack.
In daddy's car I feel quite stuck.
I have to sit still and get fed up.
The train is best, I can move about.
When we get to our stop, I don't want
to get out.

THE WASHING MACHINE

I looked into the window
And saw my socks go round,
There are a lot of bubbles
But they don't make a sound.
I caught glimpse of daddy's shirt
And also mummy's blouse,
when suddenly they all spun off
And left a sudsy cloud.
As I was wondering where they'd gone
They all appeared again,
But this time as they turned around
It seemed to start to rain.
The water it came tumbling down
And made them wet again.

SCISSORS

I need to use some scissors.
We are cutting things out today.
My teacher said she would show me.
But my fingers won't go the right way.
I push my thumb in the first hole.
And my finger should go in the next.
But as hard as I try to do this.
I find I get more in a mess.
Instead I will draw a picture today.
Yes, then the scissors can go away.

MY PRETEND FRIEND

My friend Billy was naughty today.
He took his friend's toys and hid them away.
The cars that he took were ones that I like.
I will play with them when I'm in bed at night.
I know my friend Billy is in my mind.
Mum said when I'm older, I will find.
He was someone to blame on a naughty day.
And when I grow up, he will go away.

MY PRAYERS

I say my prayers most times at night
when I go up to bed.
I wonder if He'd mind if I
save them for morning instead.

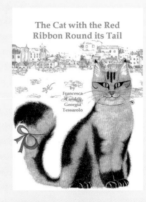